Grasp the Nettle

APPRECIATING THE BOLD LIFE OF
BISHOP WILLIAM E. SWING

Grasp the Nettle

APPRECIATING THE BOLD LIFE OF
BISHOP WILLIAM E. SWING

John W. Weiser

Project Editor: Sandra Gary
Book and cover design: Barbara Geisler Design
Copy Editor: Maureen Perry
Cover photo of Bishop Swing: Peter DaSilva
Stinging nettle image: istock/Difydave

ISBN: 9788294019113
Library of Congress Control Number: 2023906012

This book is dedicated to my children and grandchildren, who, I trust, will be inspired by Bill Swing's remarkable story.

Contents

Acknowledgments

I have been fortunate in having access to several excellent sources for this book. First and foremost are two books by Bill Swing himself. The first is "A Bishop's Quest," which recounts the formation of the United Religions Initiative. The second is "The Sacred and the Silly," a collection of wonderful and warm stories by Bill including thumbnail descriptions of several of the topics covered more fully in this book. I also had the good fortune of getting some background materials directly from Bill and having several conversations with him where he filled in some blanks for me.

I am also grateful to Project Editor Sandra Gary and graphic designer Barbara Geisler, both of whom also helped on my earlier book, "A Thousand Kisses," and in the publication of my mother's manuscript, "Elusive Haven." Sandra is the majordomo, helping to structure the book and shape its chapters. She engages specialists as needed and then gives the whole product a close reading.

Topsy Smalley, long-time librarian at Cabrillo College, helps scholars abroad find relevant materials in the United States. She was very helpful to me in digging out some hard-to-find information that gave this book more substance and color.

My wife, Sue, was married for decades to Ed Cony, a Pulitzer Prize winner and then managing editor of The Wall Street Journal. Sue was herself managing editor of The Stanford Daily. She is a careful reader and sound editor. She gave my manuscript a careful reading and made many valuable suggestions.

Introduction

Dear Children, Grandchildren, Extended Family, and Friends,

Once upon a time, there lived a remarkable man named Bill Swing.

Beginning from very modest circumstances and ranking near the bottom of his class in college, he nevertheless, through sterling character, achieved extraordinary results. Both those limitations are fully described in Bill's books "A Bishop's Quest" and "The Sacred and the Silly." Thus, he gives us our first lesson: It's not the gifts you are given that matter; it's what you do with them.

I want to tell you about Bishop Swing.

The idea for this book originated at my 90th birthday party in February 2022. Bishop Swing had been invited and had accepted. But as he learned that six of my eight children and 10 of my grandchildren were flying in from New York, he declined, deciding that all that time in airports and in airplanes raised a risk of Covid too high for him, considering his wife, Mary's, delicate health.

I wanted to tell my children and grandchildren about the bishop but had no document to give them.

Hence the idea for this book.

My writing coach, Sandra Gary, showed me many books, including several written by Bill, and some by others that contain information about Bill, and she wondered what I thought I was going to add to all that. I am happy all those books exist, so people can learn as much as they want about Bill. And I am happy those books exist because they provide much of the material for my effort. Still, they were not the handy collection of stories I wanted to share with my children and grandchildren.

I propose to write a short book of admiration about Bill. I do not intend to displace or supersede what has already been written. I intend, rather, to select some episodes from Bill's life that illustrate, in my view, Bill's strengths. I expect to emphasize episodes that particularly caught my attention, hoping to make the stories more personal and compelling. And my focus will be on attributes of Bill's character that led to great results. I also draw lessons from the stories that could be applicable to our own lives.

I chose "Grasp the Nettle" as title for this book because the phrase offers figurative advice to be bold in tackling challenges. If you grasp a stinging nettle plant firmly, you flatten out its stiff hairs which otherwise painfully penetrate your skin.

I hope this short book will be an inspiration for

you, my family readers.

Let's begin with a brief description of the man himself. Bill is about six feet tall, with clear blue eyes and the bearing of an athletic man. He has a ruddy complexion, like someone who spends considerable time outdoors. In his deportment, he is comfortable in his skin, happy to be himself. He is open, approachable, and welcoming. As you will see below, he is energetic, daring and hard-working. He also loves a good joke and seems to have no fear. William Edwin Swing was born in Huntington, West Virginia, on August 26, 1936.

I first met Bill, I believe, in 2010. I had just completed the maximum nine years on the board of the Graduate Theological Union (GTU), an institution of higher learning in Berkeley that brings together scholars from many faiths, and had decided it was time to do something else. I asked Rita Semel (a legendary interfaith bridge-builder in the San Francisco Bay Area) what she might recommend. Rita is an extraordinary person and I worked hard to have her be Vice-Chair in the eight years I served as Chair of the Board of the GTU. She said she could get me on the board of Catholic Charities or introduce me to Bishop Swing. After I heard her describe the United Religions Initiative, the global, interfaith effort he initiated, I opted for Bishop Swing.

In light of my background, I have a strong attraction to interfaith. I called him and he invited me to lunch. Along with Bill's wife, Mary, we had a long lunch and covered a lot of territory. On the way back, Bill described what became known as the President's Council of URI and asked me to be the Chair. I accepted and over the next ten years we developed a very comfortable working relationship.

Let's start our story.

1

The AIDS Crisis

B ill Swing was elected Bishop of The Episcopal
Diocese of California in 1980. His "seat" was
Grace Cathedral in San Francisco for the ensuing
26 years.

To give some context to the stories that follow,
let's recount the responsibilities of a bishop of the
Episcopal Church. As bishop, Bill must provide spiritual guidance and nourishment to 35,000 parishioners and 400 priests and deacons. That's the human
flock. There is also looking after the physical plant.
The bishop has responsibility for 40 schools, and 87
churches and for housing 1,500 homeless each night.
There is also the challenge of navigating the diocese through the political challenges that regularly
arise and raising the money to keep the enterprise
running, as well as raising new funds for expansion
and new ventures. It is very much a full-time job.

Bill tells us that up until he became bishop, he
had never had a serious conversation with any gay

person about gay issues. In San Francisco, AIDS and the gay world quickly thrust themselves on Bill's attention.

In his role as bishop, Bill regularly visited parishes in his diocese. He sensed a somber air in many of them and learned that some parishes had lost 30, 40 or even more men in their congregation in the preceding few years — brothers, uncles, sons, nephews — who had died of a new, as yet unnamed disease. These were not people on the fringes of society, but upstanding members of the community and congregants in Bill's diocese.

Then the disease struck even closer to home. A 36-year-old man named C. Wesley Hallock was working in the diocesan office, in Bill's religious household. Wesley became gravely ill. Bill visited him often in the hospital and then watched him die a painful, slow death. He was a victim of what would soon be called AIDS. When Wesley died, the disease still did not have an official name. It was called either gay cancer or gay pneumonia.

The disease was ravaging the gay population and the doctors were scrambling for answers. They had learned that the disease had a long latency period, that is, people had it for a long time before visible symptoms appeared. That implied that some already had it, did not know it, and were potentially infecting others. At a trailblazing conference that Bill organized at Grace Cathedral in 1986, Dr. Mathilde Krim, a renowned researcher, stated that at the time there were 17,000 known cases of AIDS in the US, but she estimated that there were between one and three million people infected with the disease. That implied there was an epidemic raging out of sight. Key doctors were increasingly convinced that the immune system was involved, but no one knew if the disease was caused by a virus or exactly how it spread. It was clear that if you caught it, it was likely to be fatal.

Eventually the virus that caused AIDS was identified. Then Rock Hudson, a matinee idol and epitome of the heterosexual male, announced that he was homosexual and that he had AIDS. His death soon thereafter changed the landscape — newspapers that had avoided stories about AIDS were now hungry for any scrap of information. The government, which in the Reagan years was trying to bring federal spending down, especially with funds for AIDS research, was now anxious to show the country that AIDS was their top health care priority.

Very early on, Bill was determined to learn more. He always began by listening. With the help of two priests, he rented a house on Castro Street, right in the middle of the gay community. They invited nearby residents to come by for a visit. The first few came with trepidation. Their experience with clergy had been poor. They quickly learned that Bill came with an open mind and a loving heart. Bill went there on Tuesday nights to speak to any person who would talk with him. This itself was a brave step. The Castro District at the time was beginning to resemble a battlefield; there were sick and dying men in houses in all directions. Parents, brothers, sisters, partners, and close friends were there trying to comfort those still alive, and sadly mourning those who had just died. Ambulances swooped through regularly to take those who needed to be hospitalized. Vehicles from funeral homes periodically stopped by to pick up the bodies of those who died at home. It was a tragic scene.

Bill's action was also audacious. Most members of polite society shunned the gay community and did not wish to be identified with it in any way. Indeed, Randy Shilts in his definitive book about the AIDS crisis, "And the Band Played On," tells us that one of the significant problems in the AIDS epidemic was that the major newspapers such as The New York Times and The Washington Post, whose function was to draw the public's attention to major events and to spotlight government inaction, did not wish to have their front pages sullied with the news of the gay community and its activities. Hence, they did not report on the significant number of deaths and the limited government efforts to investigate the disease and bring it under control. The gay community was off-limits to most of society. They were the lepers of modern society.

But Bill waded in.

Bill's questions to those who came to talk were: When did you first realize your sexual orientation? What was your parents' reaction? What was the reaction of your religious community? He quickly realized that most of the men with whom he spoke were refugees from other cities and towns, who had fled homes that had disowned them, communities that banished them and religious communities that ostracized them. They had come to San Francisco to be out in the open, to be themselves. This realization led Bill to see his LGBT congregants not as a mission or as a political tool, but as people in need of pastoral care not given to them by other Christians.

Having listened and reflected, Bill decided that it was time for action. In 1986, Bill organized the National Episcopal Conference on the AIDS Crisis, a nondenominational meeting of spiritual and religious leaders and medical experts to confront the epidemic. The gathering was at Grace Cathedral, and was the first religious conference in the world to deal with all the factors of the disease. Three hundred religious leaders and medical experts from 44 states and four countries attended the three-day conference. It is where researcher Dr. Mathilde Krim indicated there was an epidemic raging out of sight.

Bill ended up lecturing on AIDS around the world and was invited to become a member of the Board of Directors of the American Foundation for AIDS research. He served on the Board for 20 years.

Bill also took direct action in his diocese. Bill arranged for a special chapel in Grace Cathedral dedicated to AIDS victims. It is just to the right as you enter the front door of the Cathedral, and features a sculpture by Keith Haring.

PHOTO COURTESY OF THE WHITE HOUSE

At the White House in 1987 speaking about the AIDS crisis (clockwise around the table) President George H. W. Bush, Bishop Swing, Dr. Anthony Fauci of the National Institutes of Health, Dr. Burton Lee and Surgeon General C. Everett Koop.

Many of the gay men to whom he ministered were deeply moved by his ministry. They wanted to minister to their brothers as he had ministered to them. That posed a real challenge as The Episcopal Church was not yet ready to ordain members of the gay community. Bill tells us, "I pushed the envelope, but I played by the rules." So, he convened a group of gay men who wanted to be ordained, designed a special stole for them, blessed them and sent them out into the gay world to minister to their needy brothers. They were good men, but they had not been formally ordained; they could not administer sacraments. Still, they felt empowered by Bill to go out and serve their community. And so they did.

Bill kept pushing and eventually was allowed to ordain members of the gay community. He tells us that in time, he "had ordained more openly gay and lesbian priests and deacons...than any bishop in the history of the Christian Church. I didn't do it to fulfill a liberal agenda or out of a sense of justice. All that I ever wanted was to extend the dignity due to all human beings. To me, it wasn't a gay issue. It was a human issue."

Before George H. W. Bush became Vice-President, he and his wife Barbara had been congregants of Bill's when Bill served as rector of St. Columba's Church in Washington, DC. The doctors in San

Bishop Swing ordaining priests at Grace Cathedral
before The Episcopal Church allowed the ordination of
gay people. Boldly, he devised a unique ceremony to bless
and empower a group of gay men to go out and minister
to members of their community suffering from AIDS.

Francisco working with AIDS patients thought it
might be good for someone like Bill to educate the
Reagan-Bush administration on what was happening
at the epicenter of the disease. Bill got himself invited
to the White House and found himself meeting with
Vice President Bush, Anthony Fauci of the National
Institutes of Health and Everett Koop, the Surgeon
General. His hosts in Washington found the meetings with Bill so valuable that he was invited back on
a regular basis.

In Randy Shilts' authoritative book "And the
Band Played On," there are 600 pages with specific
details on each page. In my reading of the book, only

two people with religious background appear in it. The first is Mother Teresa who was in the United States to receive the nation's highest civilian award. On her way home to India, she stopped in San Francisco to visit the AIDS ward in San Francisco General Hospital.

The second person is Bill Swing. Shilts writes that in a "seminal sermon," Bill argued that, "If Jesus were alive in 1985, he would not be standing with the moralists condemning gays but with the people suffering from AIDS. One of the things that made Christ so compassionate was that he cast his lot with outcasts."

LESSONS

See for yourself. It is always easy to get secondhand information, but much better to learn first-hand. Bill went right to the source. Society spurned the gay community, but Bill was not intimidated.

Be courageous. For a heterosexual male, the AIDS-riddled gay community seemed daunting and unwelcoming, and members of "polite" society kept their distance from these outcasts. There had even been an erroneous message, promulgated by governmental authorities, that you could catch AIDS through casual contact. But Bill walked right into the middle of the gay residential community to meet gay men face to face.

Think for yourself. There were moralists on the right who thought AIDS was God's scourge on gays for violating God's fundamental division of humanity into male and female. You can imagine therefore why senior members of The Episcopal Church were troubled with the prospect of ordaining gay men as clergy. But, if you see gays as fundamentally children of God who did not choose, but were born with, their homosexuality, it dramatically changes your perspective. Here Bill was willing to think for himself and willing to take potential criticism from his own community to pursue what he thought was the better path. It takes courage to move against a strong tide.

Live your faith. While most professional religious men kept their distance from the "sinful" gay community, Bill reflected on Christ and then did what he thought Christ would do.

2

Formation of the United Religions Initiative

The United Nations was planning to celebrate its 50th anniversary in San Francisco in 1995. They asked Bill if he would convene the leaders of the world's religions to parallel the convening by the UN of the leaders of the nations of the world at the planned celebration. Bill agreed. As he reflected on the fact that the nations of the world had a mechanism by which they could meet to discuss world problems, he realized the religions of the world had nothing comparable. The more he thought about it, the more important a United Religions paralleling the United Nations seemed to be to him. It would be a place where religions could discuss how to deal with the world's problems, and where they could hold each other accountable. He made a vow to make a United Religions happen.

The next two years were spent planning and organizing for the UN celebration. Still, as Bill visited religious leaders to solicit their participation in the anniversary, he also sought their help with United Religions. He did well on the first count, but poorly on the second. There seemed little interest in a United Religions.

Indeed, he suffered one big disappointment. He had a warm relationship with South African Anglican bishop and theologian Desmond Tutu, and Bill believed that if he could get support from both Tutu and the Dalai Lama, he'd be off to a good start. However, to Tutu the United Religions seemed like yet another international interfaith organization, of which there were already many. Indeed, Tutu himself was busy working with two of the larger global interfaith organizations. He turned Bill down.

Work continued on the UN celebration. That was a big success.

At the same time, Bill also had a small committee working on the United Religions. They tentatively set a charter-writing session for United Religions for the following year.

After the UN celebration, Bill decided to take a trip overseas to meet leaders of the world's major religions and obtain their support for United Religions. That would take time. He arranged for a sabbatical from his position as Bishop of California.

Bill had been invited several times to preach at a large annual meeting of the Mar Thoma Orthodox

Church in southern India. He decided to take up their offer to pay his trip expenses to India and provide housing while there. The Mar Thoma took their name from the Apostle Thomas who was believed to have visited and evangelized southern India after the death of Jesus.

Their annual meeting took place outdoors with well over 200,000 people in attendance. The attendees were very well versed in the Bible and expected substantive sermons. Bill said he spent more time with the Bible in southern India than he had since seminary.

The Mar Thoma had little interest in United Religions, but they proved to be extraordinary hosts. They arranged multiple meetings for Bill with important persons of various religions across India and Pakistan, including Mother Teresa. She expressed real interest in United Religions and promised to send a delegation to the charter-writing session. Several religious leaders also seemed open to United Religions, but few committed to future action.

Wherever Bill went, he preached, spoke and was interviewed. He was always, as he put it, "planting seeds." He saw that, whatever the views of religious leaders, the ordinary lay people were in favor of inter-religious harmony.

The meeting with Mother Teresa was one of four

important meetings on this trip. The others were with the Dalai Lama, Roman Catholic theologian Hans Kung and the Oxford Interfaith Conference. The Dalai Lama thought United Religions was a good idea and encouraged Bill. But Bill reports that in fact the Dalai Lama provided little help thereafter.

Hans Kung spent a day talking with Bill about United Religions and then told Bill he had to decide whether to work with church leaders or with people at the grassroots. Each approach had its own challenges.

In Oxford, Bill gave a rousing speech calling for a United Religions. There followed a lively Q and A session, after which the audience booed Bill off the stage. He promised he'd be back with real results. The verbal abuse only fed his determination.

The indefatigable Bill estimates he covered over 100,000 miles in his United Religions trips. He had met the Dalai Lama, the head of the Orthodox Church, the Grand Mufti in Egypt, a Chief Rabbi in Jerusalem, the Archbishop of Canterbury and Mother Teresa. He earlier had met with a number of religious leaders in India. He had one more important trip — to the Vatican.

There the Cardinal in charge threw Bill's Oxford speech on the table and said the Catholic Church would never agree to work on the proposed United Religions. Jesus had commanded them to proselytize, not to coordinate with other religions, he opined. There was also a matter of pride. The Church with its 2,000-year history and its global reach could not see itself sitting at a table as equals with some relatively new, small religion. After the Vatican's decision, Mother Teresa said she would not send delegates to the charter-writing meeting. Several religious leaders intimated that they would follow the Vatican's lead. The Vatican turndown effectively finished the quest to found a United Religions.

The demise of United Religions hurt Bill and was a huge disappointment for him. The need for a United Religions seemed so obvious to him, and yet none of the world's religious leaders were ready to participate.

Bishop Swing speaking in front of a map showing some of the more than 1,000 URI Cooperation Circles operating around the world.

Eventually, Bill concluded that those leaders were so busy managing and growing their own religious organizations that they did not want to divert any time and energy to interfaith efforts. On the other hand, people at the grassroots welcomed, indeed were enthusiastic, about working across faith boundaries.

Bill's only remaining option was to go with the grassroots approach, calling it the United Religions Initiative (URI). This was a significant change. You were moving from an organization of organizations — that is the organized religions of the world, with say 50 participants — to an organization of individuals, thousands and thousands of them.

To have funds available for the start-up of a United Religions Initiative, Bill and his wife, Mary, took out a $1 million loan, signing a $1 million note.

Over the next three years, Bill hosted charter-writing sessions at Stanford for URI, the grassroots enterprise. There were eventually several hundred attendees. They created a warm and loving community, all anxious to see the birth of a United Religions Initiative, but they made little progress on the practical specifics of a charter.

Bill also had a committee looking for help on the design of the new grassroots community, and they identified a man called Dee Hock. One can see divine intervention in bringing Dee Hock to the nascent URI effort. Hock would help Bill and his team articulate a mission and vision statement for URI and help them design the structure of URI.

Hock was a remarkable man with a very keen mind. He liked, as he said, "to peel the onion," on every idea, stripping away elements until he was down to the kernel. He had led a small banking team which created the Visa credit card system and then served as CEO of Visa. The credit card system had started as BankAmericard, and had been created and managed by Bank of America for years. While it appeared to be prospering, a careful examination found many drawbacks and very heavy, unreported losses.

BankAmericard operated in the era before instantaneous electronic communication. Purchases over a specified amount required prior approval. That in turn took a series of telephone calls up the chain in the bank, sometimes taking hours. Crooks had also learned how to game the system and were regularly stealing large sums of money from it.

Hock and a small group were tasked with finding a better way. They concluded that a whole new approach was required. They discarded the old system managed by Bank of America, and designed a new membership system, where all members were equal, and all decisions were made by a majority of the members. The system was open-ended in that new members could be enrolled, and the system was very flexible. It was a bottom-up system, in contrast to the existing top-down system.

It was a hard sell for Bank of America to give up the ownership and control of BankAmericard, which the bank had originated and into whose growth and maintenance it had poured a lot of money. It is a testament to the power of the underlying idea and the conviction of its designers that Bank of America and the leading banks agreed to scrap BankAmericard and adopt the new approach. The banks did insist that Hock agree to run the new enterprise for the first few years. He actually led it for many years as Visa grew exponentially to become the preeminent credit transfer mechanism in the world.

In his fine book, "One from Many," Hock describes multiple occasions when difficult challenges arose, and all employees would be gathered to resolve the issue. Invariably, energized by a common vision and purpose, and free to bring their gifts to bear, they came up with a solution. Hence, Hock's view that this horizontal approach was the future and that the day of a hierarchical, top-down organization was gone.

Now Hock was retired and working a small farm in Pescadero, just south of San Francisco. Bill sought him out and asked him if he thought he could help. Hock said he would not help if Bill wanted to follow the industrial revolution design of top-down direction. On the other hand, he could help if Bill was willing to work with an approach more in keeping with Mother Nature where much of the decision making was made at the lowest levels. Bill said he was willing to follow Hock's lead. That was a big concession. Bill had spent his life and had great success, to the point of becoming a bishop, in a top-down system. He had authority and knew how to use it. He was now being asked to move into an entirely new world and place authority in individuals lower in rank in a dispersed network.

Hock then said that it would take years for them to work through all the elements and asked if Bill was willing to commit the time necessary. Bill said that he had a full-time job as bishop. Hock countered that if Bill was serious about the outcome, it would take years of work and wondered if Bill was willing to commit the time. Bill made the commitment. In fact, it took three years for a team of some 13 members meeting with Hock for a week every three weeks, and in between working by themselves to think through the concept and draft the founding documents.

Hock began the sessions with Bill and his team by asking them what they were trying to accomplish. That led to weeks and months of discussion and drafting. In time, they created a powerful mission statement, a charter for URI, and 21 principles to guide future action. It was very hard work because they were trying to harmonize the beliefs and teachings of many faiths. As Bill has mentioned, the concept "God" is central to the Abrahamic religions, but does not appear in the Buddhist faith. Trying to bring those two approaches together in a single statement took a lot of discussion. When the team had finished the charter, Hock turned to the form of organization for the new venture.

Hock had developed what he called a "chaordic" organization. "Chaordic" is a combination of the words "chaos" and "order." In the Visa card system with hundreds, perhaps thousands, of banks, each bank is responsible for its customers — to select them, to manage the relationship and to take the risk of their performance. Those banks are supported by one back office which records and keeps track of all the transactions. The chaos — that is, the variety — is at the edges with the banks; and the order is brought by the back office that is central to the operation.

Eventually URI adopted a somewhat similar design. There were to be hundreds, perhaps thousands, of so-called "Cooperation Circles," which would be the key operating units; and there would be one central support office to manage the network that connected all those cooperation circles. Each Cooperation Circle (CC) was to consist of at least seven individuals, among whom there were to be representatives of at least three different religions, indigenous traditions or spiritual expressions. Each Cooperation Circle selected the matter on which it wanted to work and managed and funded its work. It made its decisions independent of the support office.

The CCs met one of Bill's original goals — that URI was not to be a debating society but was to engage in real work. That fact was of great importance to George Shultz, the late former Secretary of State who was a friend of Bill's and of URI. He was a believer in getting things done. He regularly remarked on the fact that Cooperation Circles were doing real work in the field to improve their communities. The fact that Cooperation Circles had to fund themselves and not depend on funding from the support office also affected the dynamic of the enterprise.

United Religions Initiative was launched in 2000.

Bill returned to his work as bishop and (Episcopal Canon) Charles Gibbs took responsibility for managing URI on a day-to-day basis. It always seemed to me that in those days, Charles was the "glue" that held URI together. He regularly traveled the world, visiting the scattered Cooperation Circles and stitching the enterprise together with his presence. Charles' generosity of spirit and his openness

*Bishop Swing and fellow URI members building a web
of interfaith connections while enacting the organization's
"weaving the network" exercise.*

made the central office work smoothly.

Bill had tapped Rita Semel as Chair of the Governing Council. She had served for many years as director of the Jewish Community Relations Council. Through her work and simple, direct approach, she became well known and was respected by all political leaders in the Bay Area. She and Charles had been among the very small group that early on cultivated the seeds of URI. Charles and Rita had an excellent personal relationship, and both had Bill's confidence.

One day early in the history of URI, Bill entered the URI offices and realized that the staff were all good, even holy people, working very hard, but that none of them had a business background or deep organizational experience. Bill decided to find a way to bring into URI people with respected management experience. He formed what became known as the President's Council. It consisted of some 20 people from senior business positions, who often also had deep pocketbooks. Initially, they were an informal group. After ten years or so, they were formally recognized in the bylaws as an advisory committee of the Global Council, the URI managing board.

The members provided almost all the funding for URI in its first decade. One man in particular, Bill Bowes, was a very wealthy backer of new ventures. He and Bill had met when they were sitting opposite each other at a charity luncheon. Bill was curious about venture capital and asked Bowes about that. Bowes was curious about church organization and asked about that. Their conversation continued for years. Bowes became a great admirer of Bill and was very generous to URI, happy to support Bill's venture. The same was true of other "friends of Bill" who were the members of the President's Council. They had a general idea of what URI was about, but they supported URI because they knew and admired Bill and wanted to help him further his work.

The President's Council has provided good advice to Bill, to URI's Executive Director and to

URI's Chair. The majority of URI's governing Executive Committee members today are also members of the President's Council.

It's worth pausing for a moment and reflecting on the fact that over the last dozen years, Bill has brought to the President's Council a steady stream of highly qualified individuals. Like many of us, he has occasion to meet many people, but he evidences a genuine interest in them, in learning about them and from them. And they in turn soon realize he is a fascinating person with challenging ventures underway, and in time they become interested in one of his many ventures.

Today, in 2022, the URI Charter has withstood the test of time.

There are over 1,000 Cooperation Circles, in well over a hundred countries. URI has become the world's largest grassroots interfaith organization. With 1,000 units working, there are many wonderful stories. Here are some of my favorites.

One team in Africa delivered blood for transfusions to outlying health clinics. One elderly patient in need of a transfusion said he would only accept Muslim blood. The team brought over several bags of blood and said they'd be happy to give him Muslim blood if he could help them identify which bag was the right one. Soon the old man realized all the blood was interchangeable. Lesson learned.

The second story tells of a Circle also in Africa which organized a soccer game where all the players were clerics of different denominations. The stands were packed; as the game progressed, competitive instincts kicked in and soon Muslims in the stands were cheering for the rabbi as he kicked the ball to the imam who passed forward to the priest. All had a good time and interfaith relationships were advanced.

The third story is of a friend of mine, a leader of a Circle in Jerusalem. She has assembled a group of women of different religions who walk regularly in a big park nearby. They also undertake tasks such as planting new trees in an area devastated by fire. The women's garb identifies them by ethnicity, and they provide a visible example of Jews and Arabs working together.

Recently, URI had a significant reorganization with most decision-making passing through a small executive committee, of which Bill is a permanent member. The enterprise is about to inaugurate its third chief executive. It is certainly up and running, and yet great opportunities remain — to expand the number of CCs, to enrich their relationships with each other, to strengthen regional oversight and to host one or more Global Assemblies, the horizontal bringing together of many members to be a catalyst for new insights and initiatives.

URI's future is bright.

LESSONS

Don't be afraid of pursuing a good idea. In his travels, Bill met many leaders who told him that they had considered something like United Religions. Yet, it was only Bill who thought it through and then spent many arduous hours trying to make it happen.

Don't be afraid to wrestle a good idea to the ground and, if promising, to pursue it to fruition. Years ago, in my early years with Bechtel, I worked with some remarkable entrepreneurs. Their efforts were regularly frustrated, and I was reminded of those children's toys with a weighted round bottom. You can keep knocking those toys over, but they right themselves every time. So with Bill. If stopped or diverted, he reoriented himself and moved forward. He listened, learned and adjusted. In the end he made a fundamental shift and moved from a United Religions, that is, an arrangement involving major organizations to a United Religions Initiative, an interfaith arrangement involving individuals. He moved toward real possibilities and gave up tilting at windmills.

Be courageous. Early in "A Bishop's Quest," Bill writes, "I would pursue the creation of a United Religions. Although I had no idea of what a United Religions would look like, I figured that if I leapt into the arena of faiths deeply enough, proclaiming the coming of a United Religions, the answer could be discovered." This is a lovely combination of humility ("I had no idea...") and courage ("If I leapt in..."). It's typical of Bill who often undertakes initiatives where he knows he has a lot to learn, assembles people who know more, listens, and then leads, relying on their guidance.

Work hard, hold an open mind and trust the process. Just reading about Bill's trips is exhausting. He worked very hard. After a full day of meetings and discussions, Bill returned to his room to write articles for the San Jose newspaper, record the events of the day in a daily journal and then research information on the individuals he expected to meet the next day. He listened carefully in his meetings and was always ready to learn and adjust his plans as appropriate.

Be humble. Bill had been thinking and working on the idea of an interfaith organization for years, but he was ready to listen to a person he believed knew organizational patterns better than he did. So, he turned over the structuring of his creation to Dee Hock.

Put aside fear of failure. Bill does not worry about failing. If he sees promise in an idea, he plunges ahead. Perhaps it's because he does not expect to solve the problem all by himself, but rather is ready to rely on the good sense of the group he has assembled. In a baccalaureate address that Bill gave at Stanford in 2007, he urged the graduates to fail early and get it over with. "You can breathe again when you embrace failure as a part of life, not as the determining moment of life."

Above all, work hard.

3

Voices for a World Free of Nuclear Weapons

A bolishing nuclear weapons is a daunting task. You require a willing partner with whom to negotiate. Secretary of State George Shultz and President Ronald Reagan found one in Mikhail Gorbachev, then leader of the Soviet Union. Gorbachev worried about his country's ability to compete economically with the United States. Reagan had announced plans for a Space Defense Initiative. Opponents of that plan called it a Star Wars fantasy. Gorbachev believed he could not take the risk of that plan succeeding because it would effectively disarm his arsenal.

Gorbachev also wanted to avoid the crushing cost of competing with the US in a nuclear arms race. In his 1984 State of the Union message, Reagan addressed the Russian people directly and said, "A nuclear war can never be won and must never be fought." A historic summit meeting between President Reagan and Premier Gorbachev followed at Reykjavik, Iceland in 1986. The Reykjavik meeting led directly to a US-Soviet treaty in 1987 that eliminated a whole class of intermediate-range nuclear weapons.

Reagan and Gorbachev used a tit for tat basis; each country reduced its weapons in step with the other country. With that approach they substantially reduced the number of weapons that each of the two countries had.

Today the disarmament situation is much harder because there are more countries with nuclear weapons, and several countries see possession of the weapon as essential for the survival of their government. And Russia has a very different leader. Vladimir Putin is threatening the use of nuclear weapons as he sees the possibility of losing his campaign to subjugate Ukraine.

The nuclear bombs dropped on Hiroshima and Nagasaki devastated those cities, killed thousands, and left thousands more to die in time from the effects of radiation. The horrifying fact is that today's nuclear bombs are much more powerful than the bomb dropped on Hiroshima. It is not an exaggeration to say that an exchange of nuclear weapons today could lead to an end of civilization as we know it.

At the same time, there are recurring reports of "broken arrow" incidents, that is incidents where nuclear weapons are accidently put in situations where they could easily be triggered. Thus, we live with the terrifying prospect of an accidental nuclear exchange.

In an article entitled "Stumbling into a Spiritual Strategy to Combat Nuclear Weapons," Bill tells us that, "Starting in 1983, I have done what I could to respond to the existence and threat of nuclear weapons. Read books and relevant news, watched movies and TV documentaries, wrote articles, gave speeches and met with proponents and opponents of nuclear matters! Finally, in 2007, I decided to take a new tack. I asked friends of mine who are experts in this field — former Secretary of State George Shultz, Physicist Sidney Drell, former Secretary of Defense William Perry and four others — to join with me in meeting on the phone (later by Zoom) once a month to try to discover new ways of advancing nuclear abolition."

The four others were: Monica Willard, URI representative to the United Nations; Jonathan Granoff, President of the Global Security Institute; Ambassador Thomas Graham Jr.; and Ambassador James Goodby. This group was the beginning of Voices for a World Free of Nuclear Weapons. Voices is a Cooperation Circle of the United Religions Initiative. Soon after formation of Voices, Bill composed a Nuclear Prayer.

A NUCLEAR PRAYER

The Beginning and the End are in your hands,
O Creator of the Universe. And in our hands,
you have placed the fate of this planet.

We, who are tested by having both creative
and destructive powerin our free will, turn to
you in sober fear and intoxicating hope.

We ask for your guidance and to share in your
imagination in our deliberations on the use of
nuclear force.

Help us to lift the fog of atomic darkness that
hovers so pervasively over our Earth, Your
Earth, so that soon all eyes may see life
magnified by your pure light.

Bless all of us who wait today for your
Presence and who dedicate ourselves to
achieve your intended peace and rightful
equilibrium on Earth.

In the Name of all that is holy and all that
is hoped.

Amen

Bishop Swing and Former Secretary of State George Shultz, members of Voices for a World Free of Nuclear Weapons, at the Shultz home marking the publication of "The Sacred and the Silly" in 2017.

The Voices group met once a month for years to discuss nuclear disarmament from their individual perspectives. Every meeting began with the Nuclear Prayer. Later they decided to share this prayer with the world by making a powerful video, now posted on YouTube, of each of them reciting portions of the Prayer.

At the Parliament of the World Religions Conference in 2018, Bishop Swing shared the Nuclear Prayer in a session on nuclear disarmament and invited anyone interested in joining Voices to gather in a small meeting room right after the session. To his surprise, 80 people showed up. It was at this point that Voices was becoming a larger community.

In 2019, URI held the Accelerate Peace Conference at Stanford University. Bishop Swing again invited anyone interested in nuclear disarmament to join him after the session. Again, some 75 people congregated around Bill. Voices was continuing to grow.

Voices was also adding some strong players — individuals with recognized credentials in the nuclear field and community organizers.

In 2020, in commemoration of the 75th Anniversary of the Hiroshima and Nagasaki atomic bombings, four well-known interfaith and intercultural organizations — the Parliament of the World's Religions, Religions for Peace, United Religions Initiative and Charter for Compassion — came together with Voices to issue a joint statement: The Hiroshima/Nagasaki Accord. It was a coup for Bill. It was the first time these four interfaith organizations had cooperated on a common venture and opened the door for future cooperation.

The Voices Education Team helped to develop nuclear disarmament curricula geared for several age groups from children to adults. Voices has also given an annual Voices Youth Award. Three such awards have been given.

Voices also sponsored and produced a powerful

film: "The Bomb: Yesterday, Today and Tomorrow," which features former Soviet Union Premier Mikhail Gorbachev, and former US Secretary of State George Shultz sharing their personal statements and reflections on the historic Summit Meeting at Reykjavik, Iceland. The film also includes numerous world figures who have played a major part over many decades in the cause of nuclear disarmament.

In 2022, Voices, together with twelve other organizations, sponsored the First Annual Nuclear Prayer Day. People all over the world united in prayer for a world free of nuclear weapons. It was a big success with over 100,000 people praying together. The four interfaith organizations mentioned above worked together on this and were joined by eight other international interfaith organizations.

One can see Annual Nuclear Prayer Days as a way forward to building a large global constituency for a world free of nuclear weapons, with religion at its core.

Elimination of nuclear weapons is a huge challenge today. In a book issued in 1995, entitled, "The War That Must Never Be Fought," and co-edited by the late George Shultz (he was then 95), the final chapter sketches out a "joint enterprise" based on the principle of shared responsibility. Global in scope, it involves the nations that possess nuclear weapons joining with nations that do not have such weapons but have advanced civil nuclear capabilities to join in preventing the spread of nuclear weapon capabilities.

LESSONS

Do something positive. The effort of Voices, led by Bill, seems both fitting and timely. The Talmud has a relevant passage: "You are not obligated to complete the work, but neither are you free to abandon it." When faced with a huge problem, at least do something positive and constructive. Bill is leading such an effort. He is building a constituency in support of eliminating nuclear weapons, a constituency that will demand action by political leaders and support appropriate efforts by those leaders.

Educate and motivate. In "The War That Must Never Be Fought," Shultz also writes that Reagan and Gorbachev "succeeded because they provided strong leadership and because their people were ready for change." In that context, the effort of Voices also seems relevant as it educates and motivates the public to demand change.

4

Homeless in San Francisco

Today in the San Francisco Bay Area we are used to seeing homeless people on stoops, under benches or elsewhere; but 40 years ago, it was a new phenomenon. In 1980, the Mayor of San Francisco, Dianne Feinstein, called Bill to ask for his help in addressing a "temporary" problem of homeless people as winter approached. Bill agreed to do his part. The first night the Grace Cathedral complex housed 40 people. Soon the number increased to 250. But they were poor guests. After a few weeks people living near the Cathedral complained that their cars had been vandalized and that their children had to step over needles and condoms as they walked to school. Bill had to move the homeless elsewhere.

The diocese owned a community building south of Market Street. Over the years, local politicians had come to use the building as their meeting place. They were loudly unhappy about having to give up the place. As it happened those responsible for the building had been financially irresponsible and the building was dangerously in debt. Bill moved with determination. He threw out those in charge and put a tough disciplinarian in their place and moved the homeless there. As the AIDS crisis burgeoned, the authorities closed down the city's gay bathhouses. The owner of a closed bathhouse near Bill's south of Market building offered to rent the bathhouse to Bill. Bill took it, cleaned it up and soon doubled the number of homeless he was housing. Bill kept at it and soon they were using 11 locations for housing, including, for a while, a ship. They were housing 1,500 homeless every night and serving 280,000 meals a year.

*The Bishop Swing Community House
on 10th Street in San Francisco.*

When Bill retired as bishop, the diocese built a new $26 million homeless facility, the Bishop Swing Community Center. Most of the preparatory work and the fundraising for the center were done while Bill was still in office.

In 2013, the center served more than 13,000 homeless and poor individuals.

LESSONS

Be responsive. When asked for help by the Mayor, Bill responded quickly and affirmatively, ready to do his share, not looking for excuses.

Be decisive. When there were problems at the comunity house, Bill acted decisively, threw out the rascals and put in a new team.

Follow through. From a simple request to house some homeless for an evening, Bill moved on to a large center, providing a longer-term solution.

Be compassionate. Many of us, including some clergy, look away when confronted by the homeless. Bill treated them as human beings in need and helped.

5

An African American
Development Bank

On March 3, 1991, Rodney King was pursued in a high-speed chase by the Los Angeles Police. When the police finally caught King, they pulled him out of the car he was driving and several officers, with a dozen officers looking on, brutally beat him with their batons and repeatedly kicked him. They did not know that a civilian bystander with a new video camera was recording it all.

The video of white officers beating a black man became public and outraged both the black community and most whites. Later, there was a trial of the officers who had actively beaten King. In April 1992, the officers were all acquitted. In response, a city-wide riot erupted in Los Angeles that lasted for six days with widespread violence and looting. Over 2,000 people were injured and over 10,000 arrested. Both Los Angeles and the country were shaken.

Bill thought something should be done but did

not have a clear idea of what to do. He invited a group of African Americans from his diocese to his home for a conversation. They had a broad ranging discussion, reviewing the continued and deep economic disparity between the black and white communities. They did not keep minutes of their meetings, but we know what resulted. We will have to use some imagination about exactly what they discussed. Bill listened and learned a lot. He knew some of the things generally, but now he learned them more specifically and learned the commercial implications.

He knew for example that black and white neighborhoods were distinct and were not integrated. Now he learned the implications of that. Banks in both white and black neighborhoods collected deposits from residents in their areas. The funds from deposits were accumulated and then lent to borrowers and the difference between the amount of interest collected on loans and the interest paid on deposits was how banks prospered. Banks in white neighborhoods lent the funds accumulated to homeowners and to people beginning new businesses in the white neighborhoods. The banks in the black neighborhood would most often lend those funds to borrowers in white neighborhoods.

The primary reason was that most bankers were white and were familiar with potential borrowers

Bishop Swing in San Francisco, the city where he developed the possibilities of bank funding for African Americans by founding the Community Bank of the Bay.

in the white neighborhoods. Their kids went to the same schools; they belonged to the same clubs and social organizations. They knew the likely borrowers and could assess the risks. The black neighborhoods and the people living there were unknown to them. They knew that people in the black neighborhoods were poorer and that allowed them the unthinking general conclusion that borrowers there presented a bigger risk.

American commercial banks had drawn red lines around black neighborhoods and marked those neighborhoods, with the knowledge of their regulators, as areas where they would not do business. "Redlining" was a fact of life for American banking.

A black person who wanted to buy a house or a black entrepreneur who wanted to open a grocery store or a hardware store or expand his business found it next to impossible to get funds from American commercial banks.

Bill absorbed that and guided his group toward solutions that expanded the possibility of bank funding for black citizens.

Bill's group concluded that they would work to make it possible for people excluded from financing by redlining, to get a loan to buy a house or to start a business. The likely possibilities were a local development bank or a credit union. People at the meeting knew little about banks or credit unions, so two of those present were asked to investigate and report back. At the next meeting, those reporting returned with some enthusiasm. The group learned that most banks take deposits in one neighborhood and then lend those funds in other neighborhoods where they believe the prospects of making a profit are better. A development bank on the other hand is meant to keep the funds in the neighborhood in which the deposits were made. Similarly, a development bank is meant to focus on people usually locked out of the traditional financial system.

They also learned that the Clinton administration was high on development banks and saw them as a way of pulling up many depressed neighborhoods. There was talk of seeding 100 such banks around the country.

The group decided to start an exploratory effort to be called Bay Area Economic Renewal. Bill's diocese pledged $5,000 to fund the development efforts. That was huge. Front-end money is high risk and very hard to obtain. The pledge by the diocese was a big shot in the arm to the effort.

There were a number of possible ways forward. Bill's group hosted a large meeting on Fillmore Street with nationally known African American speakers. After that meeting, they decided to form a development bank.

Despite the buzz created by the Clinton Administration, there were in fact only four such banks in the country at the time. Bill's group sent representatives to visit all four banks to learn what they could. The main role model was the South Shore bank in Chicago, created in 1973 and credited with saving the south shore of Chicago from becoming an irretrievable slum. Although that bank's loans were primarily to the black residents there, its loan failure rate was better than average, and hundreds of tenants had improved their homes using the proceeds of loans from the bank.

A development bank would need substantial

capital — perhaps $5 million, the amount raised by the organizers of the Brooklyn development bank. Here Bill's group was fortunate to recruit Lyndon Comstock, who had founded the Brooklyn bank and raised the necessary funds for it. Comstock was originally from the Bay Area. He was happy with the involvement of the Episcopal diocese in the Bay Area effort because he believed participation by the religious community was essential to the success of development banks. "If they don't get it, no one else will," Comstock said.

Comstock noted that, "a large part of the bank's job will be education — explaining to residents how to take advantage of a bank, helping novice entrepreneurs draw up solid business plans and providing technical assistance to budding enterprises."

In fact, the effort to start a development bank had roots that reached further back. In the ten years preceding this effort, about 10,000 blue collar jobs had been lost in the Bay Area. Mark Friedman, one of the organizers working with Comstock on the proposed bank remembered, "When we tried to find new businesses to replace those [lost] jobs, we saw that traditional banks weren't really interested in making loans in the inner city."

So, Comstock, Friedman and their associates began looking at the model of Chicago's South Side

Bank. They eventually founded the Brooklyn bank and became important players in creating the Bay Area bank.

When the new Community Bank of the Bay launched, Bill's Episcopal diocese was an initial investor in the amount of $250,000. Catholic Healthcare matched the Episcopal investment. The City of Oakland invested $1 million. They raised over $8 million in total. Bill was heavily involved in the fundraising. He even flew to Washington to try to raise money from the Clinton administration. Unfortunately, the US government is not listed among the founding investors.

The Community Bank of the Bay has been a big success. It was the first bank to receive the US Department of the Treasury CDFI (Community Development Financial Institution) certification, which is issued in recognition of institutions that service economically distressed communities.

In 2014, the bank's loan assets exceeded $175 million, and its revenue exceeded $10 million. It has made a large effort to finance green businesses. Bank depositors can move their funds into the Bay Area Green Fund; those funds would remain as savings or checking accounts, but the depositors would be assured that their funds would be invested only in businesses or projects that are environmentally friendly.

LESSONS

Do what you can. As big a success as the Community Bank of the Bay is, no one would suggest that it solves all the issues of the black/white divide. Huge differences and inequalities remain. But remember the earlier quote from the Talmud: "You are not obligated to complete the work, but neither are you free to ignore it." In other words, there are many nearly insuperable problems existing in the world today. You cannot simply throw your hands up and walk away, saying they're insuperable. You don't have to fully solve any of them, but you do have to make some effort to address the issue. Bill's efforts fit well with that advice. He directed a small but meaningful step toward solving a major problem.

Seek help. If you don't have an answer to a challenge, seek help and listen.

6

St. Luke's Hospital

St. Luke's Hospital in San Francisco was built in 1871 and run by the Episcopal Diocese of California. By the 1990s, it was still operating, but barely. It primarily served the poor in the south of Market section of San Francisco. It was losing about $25 million a year. There was a very real prospect that, like many other small hospitals, it would have to close. Suppliers were refusing to deliver for fear of nonpayment. If doctors wanted to operate, they often had to pony up cash to pay for the supplies they needed.

Bill had come to know the CEO of Sutter Health, a Sacramento-based non-profit healthcare provider, through golf tournaments. Bill invited the CEO to lunch and golf at Bill's club.

The CEO was a devout Christian and was touched by all the good works Bill's diocese had underway, including housing the homeless, feeding the hungry and providing health care for poor people south of Market Street.

PHOTO COURTESY OF UNITED RELIGIONS INITIATIVE

*Bishop Swing engaging in the style of discussion,
strategizing and convincing that he deployed to
save St. Luke's hospital.*

Bill knew that Sutter was a caring organization, and that the CEO was a believer. So, Bill pushed hard on Gospel values and pointed out that if Sutter Health took St. Luke's under its wing, thousands of poor people would benefit.

Soon Bill was in Sacramento carrying on conversations about how St. Luke's might become a part of the Sutter Health system. There were, we are told, numerous hurdles over the next 15 years and many people became involved, but it happened on Bill's "watch." As a result, in 2017 when Bill's memoir "The Sacred and the Silly" was published, a new St. Luke's was being built to replace the old hospital.

LESSON

Plan a strategy. In scanning the horizon for a solution to the St. Luke's Hospital crisis, Bill realized that he would need a deep-pocket partner in the health care business. Sutter Health was one of the likely candidates. Bill also realized that he knew the CEO of Sutter Health and that that CEO was a deeply Christian man. So, he crafted a strategy under which he would make an appeal to that CEO based on Christian values. The appeal proved successful.

7

The Salt Lake City Olympics

In 2000, Bill received a call from a man he knew in Salt Lake City. The man happened to be the son-in-law of the President of the Mormon Church. The son-in-law said his father-in-law had asked him to call Bill and ask if Bill might be willing to help them. Bill asked for some more information. The Winter Olympics were going to be held in Utah in two years and the Mormon Church was concerned that people abroad, knowing that Utah was largely a Mormon state, might think that the Mormon Church could be using the Olympics to proselytize for the Mormons. They wondered whether Bill might help.

One must stop here and ask oneself what reputation Bill had that the Mormon Church would reach out to a Protestant in California for help on a public relations issue in Utah. One can only assume that Bill's extensive efforts to create a United Religions, including several years of very large meetings at Stanford University, brought him to the attention of the leaders of the Mormon Church.

Bill enjoys a challenge and said he would help. He soon flew out to Salt Lake City. There he learned that while half the population of Salt Lake City was Mormon, the other half was a rich collection of other faiths: Muslim, Jewish, Protestant, Catholic, Orthodox, Hindu. He organized a roundtable lunch with leaders of the other faiths and put the question to them that had been raised with him. The group had several lunches, established a warm community, and developed some practical ideas.

As Bill put it, "We mapped out a plan to address the need for interfaith rituals, the counseling needs, the hospitality venues and all the other issues that would be required of an interfaith Olympics." Note the emphasis on interfaith. Put enough emphasis on interfaith and you reduce the looming presence of the Mormon Church.

Bill says that their efforts were so successful that it served as a model for succeeding Olympics and that the interfaith roundtable in Salt Lake City was still taking place 15 years later.

LESSON

Be willing to learn. Bill regularly begins a foray into new territory by assembling people who know more

PHOTO COURTESY OF UNITED RELIGIONS INITIATIVE

Bishop Swing conducting an interfaith gathering.

about the topic than he does and by listening to them. Here he assembles local religious leaders who are living as minorities in a Mormon environment. He brings them together over a meal for what was undoubtedly an open-ended conversation. And from that conversation, an interfaith solution was crafted.

8

St. Columba's Church

In the ten years that Bill was rector of St. Columba's Episcopal Church in Washington, DC from 1969 to 1979, the congregation grew from 300 members to 2,000 members, a remarkable growth. When Bill first took over as pastor, he spent considerable time observing and listening. He noticed that many families brought children to church, and that the children were soon restless, distracting the parents. He decided to talk with Sylvia Buell, the director of the Nursery School. She had several suggestions, which Bill considered and then accepted. Sylvia suggested: Don't preach for 15 minutes; limit it to five minutes. Don't read a lesson; act it out. Let the children walk up to the altar and back several times during the service. Instead of having children put money in the baskets, let them bring food to the altar. When Bill implemented these suggestions, the children responded positively, and their parents relaxed and enjoyed coming to church.

The next step forward started when the church organist died. Bill's story is that he went downtown to a bar and hired their piano player. One suspects there is more to the story. The piano player, Bob Whitmore, learned to play the organ, but much more

Bishop Swing around the time he energized and grew St. Columba's Church in Washington DC.

PHOTO COURTESY OF GRACE CATHEDRAL

important, he had great charisma and imagination and led St. Columba's congregation into performing such works as "Joseph and the Amazing Technicolor Dreamcoat." For the church's 100th anniversary, David and a talented friend wrote a full-length musical on the life of St. Columba, entitled "The Saint," which was performed on Voice of America, on television, in London and in St. Andrew's, Scotland. The musical was also performed on the isle of Iona, where Columba had served. All these efforts involved some risk, but Bill encouraged them, believing the potential benefits outweighed the risks.

The next step forward for St. Columba's occurred when a seminarian complained to Bill that Bill had hired only 12 people to teach Sunday School. The seminarian said he could recruit another 200. Bill encouraged him and the seminarian brought in the teachers. Bill tells us that Sunday School eventually grew to 350 students and the Adult Class grew to another 350.

The fourth step forward was when David left for law school, and Bill was left without a music leader. Bill had difficulty finding a replacement. Then a neighbor told him a professor was moving from Amherst to join the Brookings Institution and that the professor's wife was a piano player. Bill called her. Even though she was not Episcopalian and did not play the organ, Bill hired her. She turned out to be a real find. Soon St. Columba's had an adult choir, a boys' choir, a girls' choir and an orchestra. In time, there were 250 people in the music department.

LESSONS

Listen to your subordinates. Here are good examples of Bill taking advice from staff. There is wisdom and humility in the guy at the top accepting that he does not necessarily have the answers, and that if he keeps an open mind, he may find answers lower in the ranks.

Take measured risks. There are also several examples where Bill was willing to take a risk to move toward a solution. There is obviously a risk in launching a new musical with a fully amateur cast, and perhaps an even greater risk in having novices write a musical, staff it with amateurs and then take it on the road! Bill oversaw all that and it came out a success. I've heard Bill say that he likes "to play in the traffic." That implies he likes to be where the action is and he's willing to take a risk.

9

The Rev. Edward Miles Blum

This book is obviously about Bill's character and accomplishments, but it is noteworthy that two people had a remarkable impact on his life. This chapter will be about the first of those people: Mr. Blum — more formally, The Reverend Edward Miles Blum. The second person was Mary Taylor Swing, whom we will meet in the next chapter.

Rev. Blum was the Pastor of St. Peter's Episcopal Church in Huntington, West Virginia, where Bill and his family lived when he was growing up. One day, when Bill was 10 years old, he and some friends were playing football on a damp, chilly day. They were playing on a field next to St. Peter's Church. Mr. Blum came out of the parish hall and invited the boys in for some hot cocoa. He also had a ping pong table available, and Bill tells us that Mr. Blum had "infinite patience" as a ping pong teacher. So, the boys learned ping pong.

Mr. Blum also had the boys joining the Boy

Scouts and the Brotherhood of St. Andrew and took other steps to get the boys organized and used to following rules. As Bill says, "No 10-year-old boy could have had a better mentor than Rev. Edward Miles Blum."

One action Mr. Blum took had a big effect on Bill. Mr. Blum got Bill to attend a summer camp. The camp was staffed by young men who were very impressive. Bill deeply admired those young men and wanted to be like them. When he learned they were in seminary, Bill decided then that he would also enter the seminary.

I can understand Bill's reaction. I attended a Jesuit high school, which was staffed in part by

PHOTO COURTESY OF BISHOP WILLIAM SWING

At about ten years old, Bill Swing (right) joined other young churchgoers attending St. Peter's in Huntington, West Virginia.

The Rev. Edward Miles Blum, who introduced Bishop Swing to a life of faith and to The Episcopal Church.

what we called "scholastics." These were young men in their late twenties, not that much older than we high school students. At recess they'd play basketball with the students. They were very accessible, but we all knew that they were on a 13-year journey to the priesthood and to life-long vows of poverty, obedience, and celibacy. That made them admirable. Many of the students, including me, thought of following their example and becoming priests. My spiritual adviser who knew me better than I did, persuaded me that marriage to Maria, whom he had met, was a better life option for me.

Bill ends several of his stories of achievements with the statement, "Nothing would have been possible in San Francisco if I had not gone into the Parish Hall in Huntington at the critical moment, to play ping-pong."

Mr. Blum also gave a sermon which had such an impact on Bill that he describes it twice in his book, "The Sacred and the Silly." In the sermon, Mr. Blum asked his listeners to imagine nothing visible existed — no Huntington, West Virginia, no US, no world — all there is, is God. Bill says he got it. "[W]hat dawned on me was the magnitude, the loneliness, the power, the self-imposed vulnerability, the only origin who is God. At a young age, when I captured a glimpse of the Source of Life, it was a sight that haunted and inspired all of my life."

We all must be grateful to Mr. Blum who cultivated Bill as a boy, and steered him into a life path that allowed him to have such a beneficial impact on so many of us.

LESSON

Be grateful. Bill is humble enough to acknowledge that he has received substantial help on his way. And humble enough to give thanks to those who helped him.

10

Mary Taylor Swing

This book was intended to deal only with Bill's public life and not intrude on his private life. Still, having read Bill's two books, "A Bishop's Quest" and "The Sacred and the Silly," one realizes that Bill's wife and partner, Mary, is an integral part of many of the stories we've chosen.

In just one example, Mary had an important part in Bill's becoming the Bishop of California. Bill had received an invitation to apply for the position, but the accompanying letter indicated that there were already several hundred applicants. There was also a 15-page questionnaire that he had to complete. Bill was happy in Washington and his children were well placed in school. He threw the questionnaire in the wastepaper basket. Mary saw it there and fished it out. She read it carefully and found on the last page a provision that said that finalists for the position of Bishop would be brought to San Francisco with their spouses. Mary brought the questionnaire back to Bill and asked him to fill it out.

Nevertheless, Bill and Mary had tentatively decided to remain in Washington. Shortly thereafter, Bill baptized Henry Kissinger's nephew. At a luncheon after the baptism, Kissinger reacted strongly on hearing of Bill's decision. "Mr. Swing, you tell me that the last two bishops of California faced real problems, while you've had some real successes. But you plan not to seek the position because your children are in good youth groups. That is not responsible leadership," he said. Kissinger's words shook both Bill and Mary and helped them decide to continue the California application process.

Bill's election as bishop of California required a big sacrifice on the part of Mary. She had built a rich network of family and friends in Virginia where she had been born and lived much of her life. Now she was asked to move to California, where she knew very few people and had no support network as she was raising two children, while Bill spent a good deal of time on the road. She handled it like a trooper.

On Bill's long trip abroad to seek allies for United Religions, Mary was a constant companion and support. As the Mar Thoma got new appointments across India, Mary was busy rearranging air and hotel reservations. When Bill lost the only printed copy of his important Oxford speech, Mary saved

Mary and Bill Swing at the demilitarized zone (DMV) between North Korea and South Korea, while marking the fifth anniversary of the United Religions Initiative in 2005.

the day by finding a copy on her computer.

She sometimes also had to act as resident censor. Bill had been working on getting an appointment with the Archbishop of Canterbury but had no success. He drafted a stiff letter to the archbishop for whom Bill had raised substantial sums of money. He showed the draft to Mary, who said it was too harsh. He redrafted and softened it, but Mary thought it was still too stiff. So Bill wrote a very courteous letter and got an appointment.

As the wife of a pastor, Mary made big contributions to Bill's success. In his first parish in Weirton, West Virginia, Mary brought her considerable hospitality skills to host picnics and dinners to bring parishioners together and enrich the life of the parish. She did the same at St. Columba's.

When Bill was bishop, he and Mary had dinner in their home with each of the men and women who Bill was to ordain. Over a 20-year span that was quite a number.

Mary also was the last resort when Bill was in a pinch. Once as he was checking in for an international flight, he realized he'd forgotten his passport. Mary to the rescue.

On another occasion, he'd led the service in one church and was en route to another church to lead the service there. There had been enough time between services to allow Bill to play nine holes of golf with the minister of the first church. As he was heading to the second church, he realized that he was still wearing his cleated golf shoes, having left his formal shoes in the priest's car. Mary to the rescue.

For ten years, Bill and Mary commuted from San Francisco to Jerusalem and then for eight more years made regular trips to China to foster companion relationships among Christians.

Mary is a woman of considerable ability. When she and Bill first met on a blind date, she was working as a mathematician for Johns Hopkins Applied Physics Laboratory on a contract to perform war games.

It was heavy intellectual work.

Mary often worked to supplement the family income. In one case, she attended UC Berkeley to obtain a certificate in financial planning and became a partner in a firm offering financial services.

When URI began, Mary was its first chief financial officer. She also hosted scores of events for friend-raising and fundraising for URI.

In the last 10 years, she has also carried some very heavy physical burdens. Over a period of three years, she lost the top of one lung to cancer, had breast cancer and radiation for that, then lost the top half of her other lung to cancer and had 15 weeks of chemotherapy. As Bill says, "Never once did she cave in to self-pity, but always kept imagining a better day." That better day did come and Mary returned to full health and once again had a full head of hair.

LESSON

Marriage is a partnership. All of us who are or have been happily married understand the invaluable benefit of a good spouse. We also know that marriage is a partnership and requires both partners to pull their weight. Bill's long and happy marriage to Mary confirms that both have done their best to make their marriage succeed.

11

Golf

In baseball someone throws the ball toward you at 100 miles an hour, intending to make you miss. In golf, the ball lies there quietly, waiting for you to strike it. It's just you and the ball. There is no one else to blame if you miss it.

I personally believe that Bill's life-long commitment to golf has significantly helped his fine career. Golf is a game in which you compete with yourself. You often play and compete with other players, but at the end of the day you are measuring yourself against your handicap. Your objective is to reduce your handicap and play at par. Par is the predetermined number of strokes that a proficient (scratch, or zero handicap) golfer should require to complete a hole or a round. A golf handicap is a numerical measure of a golfer's potential to complete a hole or a round; it is used to enable players of varying abilities to compete against one another.

Thus, the game makes you honest with yourself.

To improve you have to practice. It's all very straight-forward. That same understanding of cause and effect between work (practice) and result (a lower score) pervades Bill's life.

Bill's dad was a golf pro. So, Bill had a solid foundation, but he worked at it so that he is now in that rare group of golfers who can shoot their age — that is, play 18 holes and end with a score not higher than the number of years they have lived.

Golf is also a social game. It takes time and so provides the opportunity for conversation. The fact that Bill is a very good golfer gets him invited to participate in foursomes with well-known people,

PHOTO COURTESY OF GRACE CATHEDRAL

*Bill and the ball, competing with himself
and improving through practice.*

and so his list of important acquaintances grows and his comfort level with important people increases. He has undoubtedly developed some wonderful relationships playing golf, including with Mikhail Baryshnikov. He closed the deal on St. Luke's Hospital on a golf course, and I don't doubt that he has raised millions of dollars on golf courses.

Golf has also allowed Bill to develop a network of friends who provide occasions for fun and relaxation. Bill's book, "The Sacred and the Silly" has a long chapter devoted to delightful recollections of his golfing adventures with long-time friends.

Bill has been a fine athlete. He played American Legion baseball in high school and played basketball at Kenyon College. Those are team sports, where everyone has an assigned responsibility, and the team only wins if everyone does their part. Bill absorbed those lessons and carried them into his adult life.

LESSONS

Understand the value of practice. If you want a positive effect and can achieve it through practice, then practice.

Play sports if you can. Playing sports on a team allows you to learn how to be an effective team player.

12

A Spiritual Entrepreneur

J on Burgstone is a very successful entrepreneur who
then became a professor at UC Berkeley. He is also
the lead co-author of a book entitled, "Breakthrough
Entrepreneurship." There is a section with the title,
"Not-Quite-A-Business Example: A Religious Entrepreneur," featuring our own Bill Swing. The book
touches on several of the episodes described earlier
in this manuscript, and also includes two wonderful
quotes from Bill, for which I am greatly indebted to
Professor Burgstone.

Professor Burgstone does not seem to give us a
definition of entrepreneur. Rather he has multiple
gripping descriptions of individuals who discern an
unmet need in society, carefully develop a competitive and cost-effective way to meet that unmet need,
and then work very hard to launch that way and have
it operate on a steady state basis. Thus, we can say that
Bill's long effort to launch United Religions failed
because his target market — organized religions —

felt no need for UR. But Bill recognized that individuals at the grassroots had had enough of religiously motivated violence (often incited by religious leaders intending to tighten their grip on power by fomenting differences with others), and so Bill offered people at the grassroots a mechanism for interfaith cooperation to meet their need.

Bill describes an "entrepreneurial" moment early in his career. He was then the pastor of a tiny church in Weirton, West Virginia, a small town dominated by a steel mill. The mill stood near the church, which had earlier been a plumbing shop. The church could hold 40 people.

One day Bill undertook a daring venture. He made an appointment to see the president of the steel mill. When he arrived at the president's desk, the president let him know he was very busy. So, Bill blurted out that he was new to the church and that the church was $3,000 in debt. The president wrote a check for that amount and asked if there was anything else. Bill asked that the president and his wife come to church the following Sunday and sit in the front. The president agreed. Bill said that since the president and his wife were going to be members of the church, would he mind making a yearly pledge. Asked to propose an amount, Bill again mentioned $3,000 and got another check in that amount. With

Bishop Swing inspiring perspective and vision.

that, he gave thanks and left.

Outside, he tells us he thought to himself, "My goodness, I didn't know I had it in me. I think I am an entrepreneur. I hope God can use an entrepreneur." He adds, "At that moment my career took flight." Bill was in Weirton for six years and while he was there, the church bought three acres of land in a new downtown area and built a brand-new church building. The bishop considering Bill's next assignment recognized the drive and talent in the young priest and next assigned him to St. Columba's Church in Washington, DC, whose congregants included George and Barbara Bush. We know that Bill's next position after that was Bishop of California. That's a remarkable two jumps — from pastor of a tiny church in a steel mill town in West Virginia to bishop of California.

Bill describes his experience as a religious entrepreneur in Jon Burgstone's book, saying, "The impossibility of the task is the thing that makes it so attractive. The joy of being an entrepreneur is the hunt, the chase. It's almost an elaborate game. There's something utterly enticing, because backing down isn't an option." How wonderful that Bill was experiencing joy and excitement as he was pursuing his various endeavors. I'm happy that it wasn't all just work.

The pulpit is a lonely place. You are by yourself and below you is a large body of parishioners, hoping for enlightenment and inspiration. Bill tells us that he has given 900 sermons. The Episcopal Diocese of California has collected sermons that Bill gave to those being ordained and their families and friends. The collection is entitled "A Swing with a Crozier." There are 100 such sermons, and having sampled them, I can say that no two are alike. Each reflects a new wrestling with Biblical text and original insights. Bill puts in a lot of work on his sermons and talks.

The second quote from Bill that Professor Burgstone gives us is, "Entrepreneurs are always on a pilgrimage which finally leads to the realm of the

Spirit, the Creator and the Creation. Inexorably, one has to end up in the field of the 'ultimate'."

I find it deeply satisfying that Bill saw himself on a pilgrimage as he pursued the endeavors we've described. It is risky to try to describe another person's interior life, but it seems permissible to me to quote the observations of the person himself. The quote above seems to confirm what one intuits reflecting on Bill's life. He is a deeply spiritual and religious man, drawing strength and encouragement from his relationship with God. It seems entirely appropriate to end this short appreciation of Bill by relying on his own statement that he has all along been on a pilgrimage to the realm of the Divine. He has kept his eyes on the prize.

LESSON

Keep things in perspective and above all keep your eyes on the prize.